color
essentials

LESLIE GEDDES-BROWN

color
essentials

RYLAND
PETERS
& SMALL
LONDON NEW YORK

Designer Emilie Ekström
Senior editor Henrietta Heald
Picture research Claire Hector
Production Doborah Wohnor
Art director Gabriella Le Grazie
Publishing director Alison Starling

10 9 8 7 6 5 4 3 2 1

First published in the USA in 2004 by
Ryland Peters & Small, Inc.
519 Broadway
5th Floor
New York, NY 10012
www.rylandpeters.com

Some of the text in this book first appeared in
The Color Design File.

Library of Congress Cataloging-in-Publication Data
Geddes-Brown, Leslie.
  Color essentials / Leslie Geddes-Brown.
    p. cm.
  Includes index.
  ISBN 1-84172-687-7
  1. Color in interior decoration. I. Title.
  NK2115.5.C6G415 2004
  747'.94--dc22
                                        2004001846

Printed and bound in China.

contents

using

color

tricks of color

Color is one of the most powerful elements of interior design and decoration, but it can play all sorts of tricks on you. For example, the perception of color depends on the light: in the tropics, the hottest pinks and vermilions are at home, while cool blues simply vanish. Some colors—notably blue—recede to make a space apparently larger, while others—red is the obvious one—crowd in on the eye to make the space seem smaller. If you are trying to find your way through the maze, it helps to understand how color works and the terminology used to describe it.

When designers refer to complementary colors, harmonious colors, hues, tones, shades and tints, it is not always clear what they mean. You might think a complementary color was one that complemented another, but, technically, complementary colors are those that are the exact opposite on the color wheel. Red complements green, yellow is teamed with violet, crimson matches lime

Above Cool blues recede, creating an illusion of space in compact areas. This dining room cleverly contrasts the blue-green of the walls with a calm painting in a warmer ultramarine. The furniture and lamp both have interesting silhouettes and contrast with the walls.
Right A neat mixture of reds, orange, and neutrals avoids being overpowering, perhaps because softer neutrals and reds take up equal space in the three different widths of stripe. The whole scheme is less forceful than it at first appears.

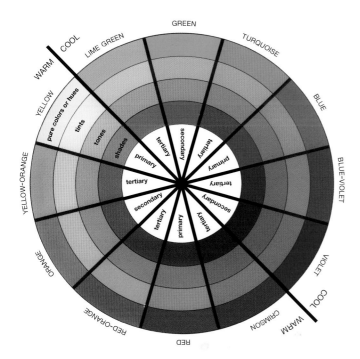

green. These colors fight each other, but a little aggression in a room scheme is no bad thing. Indeed, skilled colorists use a splash of a complementary color to relieve a one-color scheme—a vase of orange tulips in a blue room brings life and relief.

Harmonious colors are those that are adjacent to each other on the color wheel; violet, blue-purple and blue, or green, lime green, and yellow. Hue, intensity, and tone are technical terms used to describe the character of a color. Hue denotes the actual color, its quality of blueness or yellowness. You might refer to a color as lemon yellow or greenish blue, for instance. Intensity (the word "saturation" is also used) quantifies the purity of the hue, its brightness and density. At maximum intensity, it is strong and clean with nothing added to reduce the color.

When a color is dimmed or muted by the addition of a duller hue, it is "knocked back" or "dirtied." Don't imagine, however, that a knocked-back hue is by definition worse than a pure one—it is just more subtle.

the color wheel

To identify colors and use them to best advantage, consult the color wheel.

In the wheel are the three primary colors—yellow, red, and blue—along with three secondary colors, each of which is made from a mixture of two primaries. They are violet, orange, and green. Finally there are six tertiary colors, which combine a primary color and the secondary color next to it. These are turquoise (blue and green), lime green (green and yellow), crimson (violet and red), plus three nameless colors created from the mixture of orange and red, yellow and orange, and violet and blue. These hues appear on the outside of the wheel. The wheel excludes neutrals—cream, beige, brown—and black and white.

If you add a darkening agent to a primary color, you create a shade. So crimson mixed with burnt umber will be called a shade of crimson. The "shades" ring above shows the pure hues plus black. If you combine the crimson with white, it technically becomes a tint; the second ring shows tints. Tone denotes how dark or light a color is; the third ring shows tones (colors plus gray). Imagine a black-and-white photo. If everything in it were the same gray (the same tone), the whole picture would be a single blank color.

Rooms that have the benefit of strong sunlight are much easier. They can be as neutral as you please—for the sun will provide the light and drama—or they will take easily to strong primaries. Think of the sun-drenched paintings of Matisse, all primary colors, or street scenes in the tropics.

Smaller areas of sunlight—in small-windowed cottages, for instance—need to be treasured. Make sure that no drawn-back curtain reduces the light entering the room, and paint the window frames a paler color than the rest of the room to get the maximum from the incoming light.

If you can, enclose the view outside by making small sunny windows resemble pictures with ornamental frames. In such rooms, paint walls that get any sunlight a light, bright color, or hang them with mirrors to double the quantity of light. The saying "It's all done with mirrors" is particularly apposite when you are working with color and light.

color & light

Choose the colors of a room according to the quantity and quality of available light. Artists in the northern hemisphere have traditionally favored north-facing rooms because of their even distribution of light and lack of strong beams and shadows. For non-artists, such rooms need to be given excitement through color. Either white or cream will add light. But jazz up the space with touches of scarlet for warmth. Avoid too much yellow, which has become a cliché in dark or unsunny areas.

Dark rooms can be made more interesting by dark-colored decoration—especially in what are basically nighttime rooms. Spare bedrooms and dining rooms come to mind.

Above Light from unseen windows illuminates strongly colored walls, which are less obtrusive as a result. The colors also emphasize the interesting architectural details.
Opposite, left A strong light source in this spare dining room allows the use of quite dull gray-white on the walls and an even darker shade on the window shutters.
Opposite, right Light floods down the stairwell into a blue-green hall. The colors become lighter and more inviting as the stairs go up.

zoning & defining space

If you want to use color to zone an open-plan area, go for strong variations teamed with plenty of white. Work with primary and complementary colors, carefully schemed. In an overall white space, a single red wall will not only offer a warm welcome but also attract the eye. At the end of a corridor, a sheet of scarlet will beckon. A strong yellow primary on a far wall suggests a source of hidden sunlight while soft or dark blue speaks of privacy.

A large open space may get natural light from unexpected quarters. If so, make the best use of the surprise by choosing colors that stand out in natural light. White and variations of blue-white and pale blue all look stark and abstract used opposite windows; dark colors such as black, magenta, and violet change hardly at all in strong sun, while primary and secondary colors are intensified and made glowing.

Combining natural light with pale colors will automatically zone parts of an open space (you'll need to work out how to vary this after dark). You can increase the effect by varying very slightly the shades and tints on these areas. If the natural light throws one wall into prominence, making angles more evident, then let the lightest wall be in the palest shade, with adjoining walls and ceilings varied to increase the angularity. If natural light hits a white beamed ceiling, subtly color the shadowed areas with a darker shade.

Colored floors can also be used to zone parts of a space. A square of seagrass flung under a dining table will delineate the dining area from the sanded boards of the living space; boards painted black in a niche will also describe a zone used for a new purpose. Kitchens can be given soft, contrasting matting which is easy to clean, acoustically dulling, and generous to dropped dishes. It will also tell visitors that this is the cook's private space, to be entered only by invitation.

color highlights

Highlighting a room with color means using complementary hues to draw the eye where you want it to go. If you have a particularly fine view from a window, use curtains as you would use a picture frame: the curtains can be a brilliant attention-grabbing scarlet or, more subtly, a dark gray or black that highlights the colors of the scene beyond.

To signal that a room is meant for relaxing, accessorize with bright oranges, rust red, and deep browns. Chairs and sofas piled with soft throws and brilliant silk pillows in warm colors will encourage people to lounge, and the use of these bright colors will make the easy chairs the focal point of the room.

In contrast, a succession of cool tints will suggest calm and order, the highlight of the room being little more than a color slightly warmer or brighter. In a scheme of light blue and gray, a tiny touch of pale coral will do the trick without being garish. In a monochrome gray and white space, a single black object will assume huge importance: it could be a basalt vase or a black-framed photograph.

While subtle highlights suit subtle rooms, garish combinations can be ideal for certain modern interiors. Consider the primary squares of Piet Mondrian's paintings or Damien Hirst's colored circles, and you will see how it can be done. The trick is to study the bright colors of your intended highlights and control them for maximum impact.

Above Curiously, this gentle green is not an easy color to use. Here it is successfully matched with a greenish-white background, muted grays, and a touch of scarlet.
Left Pale lime-green walls bring out the sculptural shapes of the lights and chair, and encourage the abstract impression of the colored blocks of the furniture.

finding your colors

Faced with a blank room—newly plastered walls, wooden floorboards, no furniture—how do you begin to devise a decorative scheme? You may envisage the room looking good in soft blue (not least because your sofa is covered in stylish navy—and you can't afford to recover it). But what blue? What color of curtains would work, and what floor?

Start by finding a swatch of the navy sofa fabric to pin on a board. Look through paint swatches until you find a paler blue of exactly the same hue as the sofa. Buy a sample pot and paint a square on your board. Should it be darker? Is it a good color for the room or are you being too clever with your matching? If you are not convinced, try different colors: blue-gray, perhaps, or stark white.

Next, consider whether you want the room to have strong, complementary colors or ones that harmonize, such as turquoise or pale gray? Looking at other interiors in books and magazines will give you inspiration.

Then add to your board bit by bit: a scrap of fabric, perhaps, or a postcard of a lively painting. Something as simple as a bowl of apples and oranges can start you thinking. Look for combinations that work well in the food market or florist's. Clothes, too, can be inspirational, especially the work of leading designers. Don't be reluctant to copy. Artists and designers look everywhere for inspiration —and so should we.

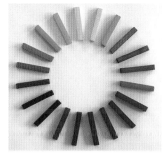

Below A swatch board is a virtually indispensable tool. Here a selection of indigo shades have been put together. There is no problem about matching these, but the mixture of textures needs to be studied; as does the small, complementary element of citrus yellow.

paint finishes

Today, gloss paint is out of fashion. We've discovered that it is unnecessary for baseboards, windowsills, and paneled doors to shine as though constantly sprayed with water. Their surface can be flat or, better still, they can have their color enhanced by the application of furniture wax. We've also realized that baseboards and doors don't have to be paler than the surrounding walls. A number of paint manufacturers work with authentic paint colors, and we've found that there's a lot more to off-white than the once ubiquitous magnolia.

A fascination with authenticity has also led to the reintroduction of all those 18th-century techniques of dragging, ragging, rolling, and scumbling (softening

Above This daring mix of lemon-yellow walls, a darker scarlet for the paintwork, blue furniture, and a dark brown door works because of the lack of pattern and ornament.
Opposite, left A marine-blue scheme is ideal for a porthole window. This bathroom is painted in shiny gloss, as though it were yacht paint.
Opposite, right Strong colors can be softened with paint effects such as dragging or ragging, or complemented with stencil work.

a color by rubbing or applying paint with a dry brush). Alternatively, it is now possible, for example, to alternate flat and shiny finishes in large, hand-painted stripes either vertically or horizontally; or different random patterns such as dragging and ragging can be used geometrically on a single wall. We've also widened our choice of colors and where we use them. A door does not have to be painted a single color that ignores its panels; different areas are colored separately, either in complementary hues, strong contrasts, or shades and tints of a single color.

Paints specially formulated for floors are a real help if you want to keep plain boards but the wood doesn't stand up to scrutiny. No amount of sanding will hide inferior soft wood, but a stain or opaque layer of paint will. If a room is dark, pickling or painting the floor a shade of white will brighten it up, while a dull area can be enlivened by a painted pattern on the floor to imitate a geometric carpet.

• Use the **color wheel** to learn what professionals mean when they talk about **complementary** colors, harmonious colors, **hues**, tones, **shades**, and tints.

• Decide what **your room** is for and how you want it to feel. Then introduce your **personal style** by **identifying** great colors.

• The **two** distinct ways of using color in an interior are in the **broad** basis of the design and as an **exciting accessory**.

• Emphasize **good features** and hide ugly ones by creating zones in different tones. It's the easiest and **cheapest way** to make an interior do what you **want**.

the

colors

naturals & neutrals

white

Until you start to plan an all-white room or area, you may not realize that white comes in as many different shades, tones, and tints as blue or green. There are whites that are greenish in color, those which are backed with blue, black, or yellow. Then, since white picks up and reflects the light, it can vary by texture. Think of a white silk velvet contrasted with a white tweed. The shadows of the hairy tweed will give a totally different overall effect from that of the smooth velvet.

Working with a pure white palette is hard but always rewarding. Hard, because it's important to consider every single element in the space. You will need to get swatches of all the fabrics, samples of every paint and, before that, have your daylight and artificial lighting worked out. It is equally important to consider whether you want gloss, eggshell, or flat paint, and where.

You can bypass some of these decisions by dividing whites into two categories: one based on blues and blacks, from bright white to various shades of gray, and the other based on browns and yellows—the beiges and creams. It is advisable to work with only one category. Currently, the grays are trendier, but the creams are always warmer. While it

Opposite, above This all-white living room brings out differences in texture, contrasting shiny white floorboards with flat walls and soft upholstery.

Opposite, below White-painted floors add extra light to any room, but all-white schemes are not always the right answer for dark areas. This living room relies on plenty of light for its glamour.

Left Although this dining area has an all-white modernism, the touch of flowery pattern for the tablecloth and the Cornish ware on the shelves immediately say "country."

Below A Swedish-inspired décor skilfully maximizes the use of light. The closets have a hint of blue to contrast with the floor, and there is blue on the sofa and pitcher.

shows dirt immediately, white fabric is no worse in this respect than black or scarlet: any pure color will mark easily. White will wash perfectly, however, because the only pure whites available in fabric come in cotton and linen. As a result, it is possible to fill a room with beautifully laundered white fabrics that are slightly scented with fresh air and cleanliness.

For kitchens, there are lots of plain white dishes available, while plain transparent glasses are honorary whites. Look at minimalist John Pawson's views on kitchens to see how white on white can work in even the busiest cooking area. White china, glass, brushed steel, and plain marble tops are allied with neutral floorboards and quantities of white cupboards.

Above Pure white is used almost without interruption. Yet this is an exceptionally well-lit room—white needs light to flourish. Note also how the perspective of the floorboards adds to the overall length.
Left If you believe in all-white bedlinen, then consider an all-white bedroom. This calm décor combines smooth textures on walls and curtains with the clean rumples of the bedside lamp and sheets.
Opposite, top and center left All-white schemes always benefit from the use of interesting shapes.
Opposite, bottom left Pure white rumpled fabric shades are the perfect foil for green vistas.
Opposite, right White needs plenty of discipline. This kitchen corner has been carefully styled with gleaming steel pitchers and a matching foil packet.

• The textures and tones of white **evoke a calm** and freshness that are at home in **city** or **country**.

• In a white room, everything fits in with **everything else**: when **you want** to rearrange it or buy more, there are **few complications**.

• Introduce **exhilaration** to a white kitchen with piles of **lemons** or **tomatoes**, boxes of earthy potatoes, and braids of creamy **garlic** bulbs.

• White is so **clean and pure** that it is the perfect antidote to **strong color**.

cream, beige, & brown

Warm, friendly, and rich, the color cream evokes heavy cream, whipped cream, thick cream. In excessive quantities it can be indigestible and sickly. It is also somewhat bland, so if you opt for a cream scheme, pick your room carefully. Even more than white, cream is a nothing color that disappears, a soft background on which other elements stand out. If you are lucky enough to have huge windows, a wonderful view, or columns and moldings, cream can work well. The larger and lighter the room, the darker the cream can be.

Cream is excellent for paneling, especially if you use several shades together. To make the most of light in the room, paint the largest flat areas in the lightest tone, using darker shades for the moldings and surrounds. If the room is very light and needs more warmth, then the reverse is true. It looks good, too, in small rural rooms, whether living areas or bedrooms in tiny cottages. In this case, the tone should be of a single

cream, a warm white that will hide the lumps and bumps on an old wall or make the most of the light emerging from little windows.

If you want to be really old-fashioned in a stylish way, give your kitchens and bathrooms cream schemes. Huge square bathtubs and washbasins should be surrounded by cream tiles and lots of built-in mirrors. Piles of fluffy white towels and a soft cream marble floor are the stuff of Hollywood. Kitchens should have a vintage cream stove with lots of those curvy kitchen cupboards so popular in the 1950s and a retro refrigerator.

Perhaps the most successful way to start using cream in combination with other colors is to think of it as an off-white. Like all such hues, cream responds well to a monochrome treatment—cream and black is extremely

Opposite page Three ways of using color to create an abstract effect: a bar of brown is painted along the wall; random beiges decorate closet doors; and a horizontal throw takes up the powerful silhouette of the mirror beyond.
This page Cream and brown used as ornament: Japanese motifs combine with brown strips painted on the wall; a decorative table is teamed with a brown-trimmed throw; shiny cream jars on a duller flat wall and somber stripes on window-seat cushions all contrast with the nuances of the neutrals.

Right Wood is a natural ally of all neutrals, and the dark counter area serves in this well-organized kitchen to create a punctuation line in an otherwise cream décor.

Below The textures of brown tweed are skillfully mingled on this painted wood sofa.

Opposite, above The abstract feeling of this modern set of rooms has been created with nothing more than an arrangement of plain wooden doors, cupboards, and a slatted blind. The strength derives from the strong dark brown of the wood allied with cream paintwork.

Opposite, below Natural leather is another ally in a neutral design.

sophisticated, as is cream combined with the deep browns of ebony and mahogany, but only one at a time. It also looks splendid combined with another single light tint: coral, sky blue, or even gray, each dulled down with the addition of white or black to the original color. The second color should not be obtrusive, but should simply add richness and a focal point to the room.

Again, it is advisable to use only one single color with the cream. White is probably the easiest because you don't have to choose it carefully to fit in with the red or yellow base of the cream. From soft voile curtains to firmly woven rugs, it can hardly be beaten.

Happily, there is no more nonsense about men's dens and women's boudoirs, and brown is at last being used as it should be. It is a color as strong and powerful as black, though rather more friendly. It is also one of the most natural colors. We are therefore very at ease with brown, which is considered warm and relaxing. Brown and beige are the colors of every wood, from the darkness of ebony, red of mahogany, tan of oak to beige of beech and birch. The more tropical the wood, the darker and firmer it gets.

Brown and beige are excellent backing colors—waxed oak and elm floorboards, pickled old paneling and log-cabin ceilings. Objects placed against brown or hung on beige walls respond with glowing gilt frames or silhouettes firmly outlined. As in nature, it's almost impossible for different kinds of

wood to look unhappy together. Brown and beige are natural in fabrics, too. Unbleached linen is a soft beige, wild silk comes in a charming range of pale tans, while natural wool from rare-breed sheep emerges looking just like the animals. Bear in mind, too, the camouflage colors of zebras, giraffes, tigers, and leopards—there are excellent manmade copies available.

The beige-brown range can be exciting, exotic, warm, and intimate as well as strong, minimalist, and mannered. It's up to you.

- If you have a room with **something special** about it, consider **cream** in all its **tints and shades**.

- The **best lighting** in a cream room is an overall glow **heightened** with **stronger beams** to show up interesting areas.

- Beige and brown are fine **backgrounds** for really strong, **stinging** colors such as brilliant blue, lime green or shocking pink, .

- Despite its **strength and presence**, dark brown is still a **neutral hue**, while beige is the neutral par excellence. Both are very **forgiving** to work with.

Opposite, above Pattern has been introduced here in the form of shiny circles on a matching flat brown wall along with the painted bricks behind.

Opposite, below left A dark, almost olive brown makes an exciting contrast with the white china and heavily grained wooden floor.

Opposite, below right An all-neutral design is enlivened by the woven sofa and slatted blinds.

Left and below The concentric squares on the bedspread pick up the color of the blond wood walls, while the texture of the matting is emphasized by the bland brown extended headboard.

gray & silver

Grays come in all kinds of variations—pink-grays, blue-grays, yellow-grays, and brown-grays—and, as usual with colors, it's best not to mix them. Although blue-grays may be considered cold, the near-ubiquity of central heating means that the idea of warmth is less important than it used to be, especially in urban areas. Silver and gray can add space and sophistication to town houses, especially those with period features such as marble fireplaces (often gray themselves), cornices to offer a variation in detailing, and ornamental doors. Subtle changes in the shade of gray can be used to highlight these features.

Gray and steel are almost essential in minimalist urban homes, from all-aluminum kitchens whose only decoration is shelves of glasses to bedrooms made comfortable by using textured gray flannels, cashmere, and faux fur. Country houses

Above A heavy black background is the perfect foil for the patterned table and brilliant green leaves.

Left The gamut of whites, grays, black, and taupe mixtures is used to create a harmonious open plan room. Sculptural objects show up well in such a scheme. Note the absence of extraneous pattern.

Opposite, above A combination of various white and black objects enlivens this small corner.

Opposite, below left and right Two views of the same area show how skillfully the grays are mixed. The central band of black and white marble unites the stone dining room with the greige living room.

perhaps should be decorated with warmer grays—the colors that hover between beige, bone, and string, and are more allied to earth tones such as burnt umber and sienna, which chime well with the rural landscape.

One great advantage of these colors is that they are extremely easy to live with. If you are starting out with a new house, uncertain about decor, you could paint the rooms in grays and live with that until you have formed more long-term ideas. Do a room at a time, leaving the surroundings gray until you have decided on something different.

Since gray and black are pure and cool by nature, they make a perfect foil for the full-strength saturated primaries: brilliant scarlet, bright yellow, or dreamy ultramarine. You can even use them with complementary colors, to provide clear, uncomplicated areas between the different hues.

Contemporary architects like these shades because they flatter architectural details. This means that, in addition to modern interiors, 18th- and 19th-century rooms can also benefit from their attention. Gray is a superb foil for gilding since its coolness flatters the richness of gold—look, for example, at the paneled rooms of French chateaux. Its use makes walls appear to recede, which is valuable if you are positioning single focal points of strong color. This may be no more than a single jungle leaf in a vase or a curvy 20th-century scarlet chair. Against the gray, it will immediately attract attention.

- Use **several shades** of gray to give **decorative** emphasis to paneling, moldings, and other **architectural** details.

- Gray is the **perfect foil** for metallics. Silver frames add **glitter**, while duller zinc and aluminum **echo its colors**.

- Gray goes well with **strong primaries**, but in an all-gray room a **subtle touch** of soft pink or blue will appear more **strongly** colored.

Left and below A steel bathtub is the central feature of this bathroom, but the mosaic tiles behind it are a subtle way of introducing pattern and texture. The temptation with such an elegantly planned room is to keep even gowns and soaps in the same colors.

Opposite, above Natural light is used to pick up the shapes of this selection of white objects placed on a white wall. Varying shades of gray and brown give extra depth.

Opposite, below left Radiators, carefully chosen and colored, can be interesting in their own right.

Opposite, below right A steel-framed chair looks perfectly at home in an otherwise white kitchen.

naturals & neutrals can be

Neutrals do not appear on the **color wheel**. They are a complex **amalgam** of many hues.

Match neutrals on a shade board, **keeping** blue-, pink-, and yellow-based **versions** apart.

combined in quantity

Texture is crucial when it comes to neutral colors—add **swatches of fabric** for **upholstery**, carpets, and curtains to your **shade board**.

Always use **test pots** of neutrals to achieve the right mix but, compared with strong colors, **smaller** test-painted **areas** will be enough.

green

Restful and pleasant, green is a good color to work with because it offers large variations of hue, shade, and tint. Curiously, the two ends of the green spectrum can live happily together, which is not the case with most other colors. Turquoise, at the far blue end, and lime green at the yellow, can be teamed as long as one is firmly knocked back. On the other hand, it's hard to mix shades of green. While racing green, at the deep end, and emerald or malachite can be put together, a mixture of dark and pale green recalls school corridors, hospital wards, and other unfriendly institutions. Worse still is the same in gloss.

As an essentially cold color, green is not ideal for a bathroom. Conversely, it works well in hot rooms such as a solarium. It is effective in urban interior schemes, which need as much connection with nature as they can get, and it is excellent with complex detailing. Green looks best on paneling, on classical cornices, or with special features emphasized by a different shade or gilding.

In the 18th century, green was an extremely expensive color to make and, as a result, became highly fashionable. The smartest pea green can be seen in many an authentic aristocratic town house, whether in London, Paris, or New Orleans. Now that paint colors are all the same price, you can achieve the look at an unfashionable fraction of the cost.

cool colors

Opposite Dark green, like navy, is a life-enhancing color and easier to control than you might expect. Here, the owner has added a wild touch of crimson carpet.

Left A complex mixture of olive green and yellow on the chairs' upholstery is strengthened with the malachite green of the plant in the foreground.

Below left The black lines in this shiny tiled floor make the softer tone seem more green than gray.

Below center and right Bright green is exciting to use, but needs to be deployed sparingly.

Dark green is ideal for 15th- and 16th-century interiors, partly because its somberness suits the heavy architecture, beamed ceilings, and small windows of the period. Tudor rooms should have the dark green painted in a flat oil which is then lightly waxed. Eighteenth-century walls may be dragged, scumbled, and combed, for this, along with pea green, was the chic 18th-century alternative to wallpaper.

Pale jade and grass green are more lively and work well in modern spaces without architectural detailing. These colors, too, make fine emphasis points set against a darker (or lighter) shade of green. For immediate impact, take a dark wall and put a jade Chinese sculpture against it—carefully lit to show its translucence. Use a grass green Venetian bottle or quilt and put it in front of the palest green wall to the same effect.

- **Dark green** walls provide a stunning background for paintings, especially hefty **oils**.

- Avoid green **gloss on walls**, mantelpieces, and doors. Flat and **eggshell** work much better.

- **Bright green** patterns on a white ground **freshen** a dull area. They can be used in wallpaper, **curtains**, and **upholstery**.

Above and right Busily patterned wallpaper should be kept carefully under control: this room uses an abstract floral with matching white and green walls.

Opposite, left White woodwork is not fashionable, but is needed here to give strength to the soft, friendly green of the walls. The wooden stair treads are important, too.

Opposite, above right A determined green is an excellent background for pictures. Frames of silver, black, and gold are all improved by it.

Opposite, below The modern painting pulls this scheme together by combining the various colors used throughout the room. This is an easy trick to pull off.

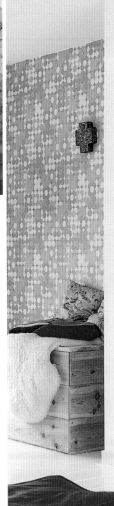

Below The combination of blue and white is only a cliché because it works. The tablescape shows blues at their most subtle.

Right The cliché can also be overturned by using blue and white in new directions. The white target circle with its lime-green eye makes a startling contribution in a period setting.

Opposite, above Soft greenish-blue is a color that is happy both indoors and out. Here it appears in a garden room by a back door.

Opposite, below The purest sky blue is at ease with both marble and brushed steel.

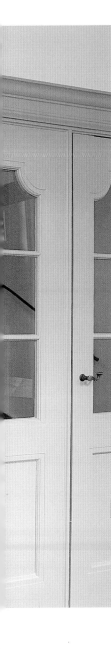

blue

Blue is the color of infinity, the clear sky blue magically created through millions of miles of empty space. It is the color of distance, faraway moody blue hills, lakes miles deep, the sea, and misty mornings. Blue is also a color used in those pictures many of us love best: the blue of a Tuscan sky behind the blue of the Virgin's robe in a Renaissance masterpiece, the Mediterranean dashes in a Matisse windowscape, or a Dufy racing scene, the blue Mark Rothko abstracts. And then there are the blues found in all the best palaces from the stinging tropical tints of India to the mirrored pomp of Versailles.

A truly adaptable color, blue ranges from warm and lively at the ultramarine end of the range to cool and breezy at the Prussian and indigo end. While it is not advisable to mix different ends of the blue spectrum, within each hue there is an enormous variety of shades and tints. Blue mixed with white varies from the palest, near off-white to a stunning range of cerulean and French blues; combined with black, it offers subtle blue-grays to the darkest midnights.

All these combinations can be arranged together—think how indigo and denim work as clothes, from the palest washed look to dirty denim. You can use ethereal blue as a background and pose dark navy against it, or simply contrast the pale tint with a duller, knocked-back gray-blue. Blue with blue in

patterns is almost invariably successful. Think of stripes and checks, tickings and wax-resist batiks of indigo, or of the more complex toiles and single-color floral chintzes. You may use them as fabrics, but you can also find them turning up as wallpaper and even carpets. Use mixes of blue on furniture, too, especially in the country or if you are beside water.

Many successful blue combinations have a maritime link—draw on the many tones of the sea on a sunny day, and pair blue with green or yellow to create intimations of a beach. Blue and white is so common in everything that it's almost a cliché, but it still works wonders. Blue is happy with almost any other color as long as the values of the respective colors are carefully controlled.

Right The plain white niche in the wall with its lone piece of china is made to work as an abstract piece of art in this minimalist room.

Below A combination of textures makes a cool color more friendly.

Opposite, left Random mosaic tiles not only pick up every other color used in the bathroom, but also add a helpful element of pattern.

Opposite, right Despite being a strong color, blue recedes. Using the lightest blue in the distance and the strongest in the foreground enhances the sense of space.

• **Blue and white** objects, from china to towels, can help to **coordinate** a scheme.

• To **calm** the whole, add black, gray, or **yellow**, in the form of paint or found objects such as **pebbles**.

• **Metallic shades** of silver look great with blue: silver frames, **steel** banisters, and **iron** buckets, for example.

• Blue responds to **geometric** patterns such as two-tone **wide stripes** and gingham.

lilac & purple

A clear range of lilacs, pinks, and purples was not invented until the mid-19th century, so the colors were rarely used historically. That makes the selection among the most modern and one we have yet to appreciate fully. Drop the majesty of imperial purple and think of these hues as black pansy, blueberry, and lavender. They can be paired with orange, ebony brown, and malachite green as long as the two are not the same tone. In general, lilac is as adaptable as pale blue, and dark purple as adaptable as midnight blue.

Lilac and pale pink often live well together, but mixing them with other shades can be difficult. The best neutral to mingle with lilac

is a bluish-gray. It doesn't matter how dark or light the gray is, for lilac is very amenable. Charcoal makes a fine contrast with a pale, dreamy lilac, but so does the palest silver gray. Black is another successful mixer. Take gray farther into the blue realm and it should be happy, especially with lilac and mauve, though the mixture will be recessive and cold. Warm up the lilac by adding a tan at the gray end of the spectrum—pale

Above and top Color boards are essential when you are combining apparently clashing colors.
Left Working rolls of fabric are used to add sugar-almond shades to the office.
Opposite, left Strong pinks and purples intensify in narrow spaces, so one colored wall is enough.
Opposite, right Rough, slubbed silk, in shades that are almost the same but subtly varied, make two chairs into a statement.

pickled boards or furniture would be fine, but take care with chestnut brown. The lilac end of the blue range has a natural affinity with steel, making it ideal for kitchen areas with lots of steel equipment.

Think of purple as a reddish navy blue and treat it as an imposing, unconventional shade. Keep it for nighttime rooms, from dining areas to bedrooms, where it is surprisingly cozy. A truly dark purple is nearer black than either midnight blue or darkest green, since its basis only hints at color. A dark purple can vary from near ebony to almost navy, and these shades should be treated differently. Both look luxurious teamed with white or with silver and steel. Gray is a great neutral at the blue end, and stone or bone the perfect foil at the brown end. So are faux furs and other textured browns and near-blacks.

But purple can also be combined with the most surprising and brilliant colors, such as orange. A strong clear blue—Chinese blue or cerulean—could replace the orange with the same vibrant effect, as could a simple grass green, a touch bluer than lime.

Since black is rarely found in nature in its true form, most of the dark, recessive shades are, in fact, deep purple, which are often used by gardeners to add background weight to colorful beds. Anyone who longs to use purple could with advantage visit gardens famous for their use of color or could look at the work of modern horticulturalists at garden shows for some idea of purple's properties.

• Don't be frightened of **lilac** and **mauve**. Call them **hyacinth** or lavender to make them more **friendly**.

• Lilacs, **always clear**, range from strong violet to **softest** mother-of-pearl. **You can team** all of them together.

• Dark purple is as **adaptable** as navy. It is **excellent** with white (and less clichéd) and **perfectly at home** with **brilliant** orange or pink.

Opposite Muted walls in a paint-effect finish in a darkish room are the backdrop for an extraordinarily bold use of shocking pink with yellow, brown, and rust.
Left By contrast, this understated living area relies on the palest of pinks and lilacs to glow against a white-on-white backdrop.
Below Color can be added—and changed—with subtle use of flowers, fruit, and added fabrics.

black

You have to be brave to choose black as the principal part of a scheme, for it has scary connotations: of night, death, and the devil, of claustrophobia and caves. A background of black unrelieved by other colors seems to suck much of the life out of a room.

Another option is to use black on a single wall and combine it with lighter tones of gray or soft, charming colors such as pale coral, sky blue, or shades of violet. Black also works on a single wall covered with pictures or collected objects (but not just black-and-white photographs, since the contrast is too strong). Flat blackboard paint can look effective on single walls that are then used for graffiti, notes or—for the confident—large sketches and diagrams. This is an attractive concept because it is so versatile, and can be especially effective in children's rooms.

Black may just work in a corridor or on a dark landing where rooms open off with an explosion of color, or in a show-off dining room used only at night and for entertaining. In fact, it is the epitome of a show-off scheme: people only use black when they want to provoke gasps of astonishment and the affectation of drama—which is why it is a nightclub color.

Black and gray make great backdrops for other colors, and they are good at defining an object's shape. Place a white sculpture against a black wall and its details are emphasized. Even more striking is the way black and gray, by their strength and discipline, mix well with the odd undisciplined object—an indoor tree or a glass of curving tulips.

- **Black** may have a background color—try **matching** blacks and you will see they can verge towards **blue** or **red**.

- Black is **hard** to use in large **quantities**. Keep its drama to a single area, and **counter it** with gray and off-white rather than **brilliant white**.

- Many newly designed **contemporary** homes are given black and gray backgrounds because they suit the **clean lines** and **uncluttered spaces** of 21st-century style.

Opposite, left This mix of plain and sculptural blacks only works with a strong light source—here invisible—and a glowing wooden floor.

Opposite, right A bright, splashy panel design rescues a black bathroom from gloom. Both glass basin and white lavatory are enhanced by the background.

Left Using black on the floor adds drama, especially when it is shiny, but the room requires lots of light. The single black piece of furniture needs a good silhouette.

Above If there is an artist in the family, create change by using blackboard paint.

Gentle and subtle changes of cool color in uncluttered spaces **induce** a feeling of calm and **pleasure**.

Combined with other colors, purple loses its daunting **majesty** to **become** a modern spice for stark spaces.

a space seem larger

Green can sometimes be a cold hue, so combine it with **warmer** colors such as coral or **rosy beige**.

Blue responds to **geometric patterns** such as two-tone wide stripes and **gingham**.

The gray-greens—**sage, olive, and celadon**—are ideal for painted furniture.

●

Gray can be combined with **strong primaries** but, in an all-gray room, **a subtle touch of blue** will appear more strongly colored.

warm colors

yellow, orange, & gold

Yellow is one of the most approachable colors—perhaps because it is capable of extraordinary variations and because, at its deepest and strongest, it never gets dark. It is also a helpful color, even in huge areas, because it intensifies much less than reds or blues, making it good on narrow stairways and in small spaces.

Use yellow for the grander rooms and those where you want to relax. It is equally satisfactory in town or country because it is associated both with classical 18th-century design and with rural cornfields and thatch. It is for living rooms and kitchens, for halls and stairways. It is lovely in a generous bedroom and, because it is friendly, in children's rooms.

Yellow is always warm but the redder the mix, the warmer it gets. The eggier end of the spectrum can be hard to work with, so it is safer to pick the sharper, citrus tones of the greener yellows—these are brighter and fresher, but less cozy.

Opposite Think unconventionally when using color, especially with the less challenging shades. Horizontal bands of sulfur yellow, beige, and rust are allied with bright green in a living room.
Above Or you can paint bold patterns directly onto the walls by using carefully cut templates. The target is a gentle mixture of white and pale grass green.
Right Never underestimate the impact of mobile objects such as this row of gold candleholders. Such arrangements can totally alter the feel of a room by changing the emphasis and focus of attention.

Right Bright orange in small doses can make a display feature of a dull corner. Here, an old cupboard has been lined in a geometric orange paper to make a crazy, clashing backdrop for an assortment of tins.
Below right Brick, terracotta, and olive shades combine particularly well with fresh primrose yellow.
Below Natural wood floors always lend a calming note to strong color treatments. Here bright orange framed by cream and yellow makes a welcoming modern room.

Opposite, left The colorwashed wall in this Italian kitchen has been finished with a warm yellow glaze and sealed with clear varnish.
Opposite, right A strip of tiles keeps apart two yellows in this room: the walls are mustard orange and the cupboards a clear bright yellow.

One drawback is that teaming yellow with other colors must be done with subtlety and sensitivity. Yellow is excellent with white and gray, and it works well with wood and neutrals, but with red or blue it needs to be carefully controlled. A bright scarlet is fine with yellow, but crimson is deadly.

Like yellow, orange is a friendly color in practical areas like kitchens and children's playrooms. But, like red, its other component, it demands attention—use it discreetly if you want glamour allied with calm, or take full advantage of its natural drama.

One way to control doubts when working with orange is not to call it orange. Think of it as terracotta, Seville, coral, or cornelian. At once it can adapt to various international styles. It features greatly in the tropics, and many "ethnic" rooms benefit from knocked-back orange walls against which can be arranged wooden Buddhas, brass elephants, ornate mirrors, and colorful textiles.

Orange is surprisingly helpful mixed with other colors. It's just a matter of making sure their values do not collide and scream. Many natural woods and fabrics are basically very knocked-back oranges, so they will look comfortable together. This goes for all the cream, bone, stone, and tan colors.

Metallic gold is marvelous to work with, though it must be the genuine article, laid on in minute slivers and veneers as gold leaf. "Gold" in decorating also takes in various other glittering metallic colors: brass, which is shinier; light bronzes, which tend toward darker brown; and old gold, which occurs when the metal has lost its shine through age. Used in small amounts on frames, in furniture, or on paneling, gold is both chic and elegant. It also looks fine with other metals—silver, aluminum, and zinc.

Trouble comes with gold used as a color rather than a metal. "Gold" and old gold in paintwork can be murky and eggy, having both the unsatisfactory qualities of yellow and brown. But, like orange, it will be happy with the brown, cream, and stone range of neutrals where, if you are clever, it will begin to look like very old, faded, and genuine gold.

- Yellow is the **friendliest color** in the spectrum, bringing warmth and **light**.

- Orange is effective with primaries and **other strong colors** in unfussy rooms.

- When using gold, think **soft olive, tan, or cream**, and if you can't dull the overall color, reduce its impact with plenty of **near-gold shades**.

pink & red

Shocking pink is similar to cerise—in theory the color of a cherry, but in fact much more blue. A tint paler is rose, a favorite with 20th-century country-house owners and, as such, something of a cliché. But combine rose with other pinks, and you will achieve an extraordinarily modern effect.

So, pinks are by no means as mimsy as we make out. Put together cerise, shocking pink, and rose, and you will have a room that narrowly avoids clashes—but the narrowness of the escape adds to the thrill. More calmly, you can take rose as the strongest color of the mix and add pale mother-of-pearl and a hint of sherbet. It will still work and looks especially good with plenty of pattern.

The problem with pink is that the yellow end of the red spectrum looks appalling when teamed with the blue end. Clashing can be as bad among the softened pinks. It is therefore crucial to work with a color board or, even better, with a corner of the designated room. Pinks, like reds, have a habit of intensifying when used together, so what looks fine in small swatches can become awful in large.

Red signals danger, and that's exactly what it means in decorative terms. The more red you use, the more it intensifies. Strong red walls turn white paintwork pink. They crowd in, enclosing you as though in a womb. Red is also a clichéd color, especially in dining rooms, where it rarely works, and libraries,

Above Kitchens are not intended to be restful, so they can carry color mixes that would be intolerable in, say, a bedroom. The shocking pink of the walls and cabinets is dramatic when mixed with the strong purple chairs and floor. But note: no other color is visible.

Opposite, above Strong architectural shapes of Bauhaus furniture and typical reds, blacks, and whites of the modernist movement are carefully juxtaposed.
Opposite, below The wonky legs and cord of the eccentric lamp lighten the drama of the floor.

which it suits better. The positive side is that, subtly used, its shades and tints are powerful and memorable. Use red in rooms where there is little wall space because of shelves, windows, or cupboards—or in enormous spaces, such as warehouses, lofts, or billiard rooms, where you want to bring the walls forward and make things a bit warmer.

If you are designing a room with red walls, choose the hue carefully. Brighter scarlets can be too dramatic for comfort, while deep crimsons are gloomy. Since red is such a thug, not only with other colors but with itself, it asks for the simplest treatments. It is not, for example, a good idea to use a large palette of colors in a basically red room: this not only looks

messy, but also dilutes the whole point of using red. You want drama, not confusion.

Any neutral is possible with red, but the one that goes particularly well, especially if you are working on a deliberately dark and emphatic room, is black or off-blacks such as ebony and charcoal. Groups of monochrome photographs are effective on red walls, while good modern furniture, especially in black leather, will be equal to the force of the walls.

Deep lacquer red is excellent in 16th- and 17th-century rooms, which were generally somber and ill lit. The color, much used during that period, well suits the dark oak furniture of the Tudors and the foxy red grain of walnut that succeeded it in fashion.

- Team **shocking** pink with **neutrals** such as charcoal, gray, **black, and beige**, but never bright white.

- If you keep to a single **hue of pink**, you can mix in quantities of **different** shades and tints.

- Use strong reds as **accents** in neutral rooms. A bunch of scarlet **sweet peas** will have an effect out of all proportion.

- One of the most **successful** combinations with strong red is a **silver** metal—one of the colors in **the range** from aluminium to zinc.

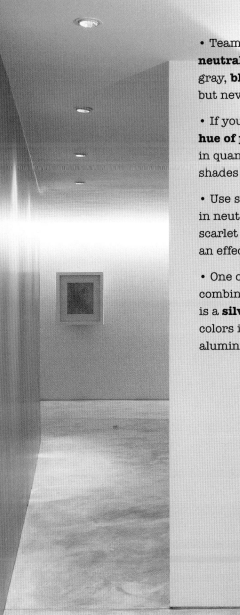

Above Feminine pink is deployed with masculine abstraction.
Left Pink's tendency to intensify in narrow spaces has been used to advantage in a friendly corridor.
Opposite, above The contrasting tile grouting makes the ranged black pans into sculptures.
Opposite, below left A mixture of woods and weaves is strengthened by the use of the plain, strong red bulk of the sofa arrangement.
Opposite, below right Red-lacquered walls and an orientally inspired abstract bring an Eastern element into this sitting area.

warm colors are

Pinks, like reds, have a **habit** of **intensifying** when used together.

Yellow is always **warm**, but the **redder** the mix, the warmer it gets.

Pure orange in small doses grabs **attention**. It's good on shiny surfaces such as **silk or glass**.

cozy and welcoming

Dulled oranges are the colors of the landscape. Use **earth** shades **inside,** but change their tone.

Red is a **nighttime** color with a need to **dominate**.

suppliers

Benjamin Moore Paints
51 Chestnut Ridge Road
Montvale, NJ 07645
800-334-0400
www.benjaminmooore.com
Over 1,400 colors, including
historic styles.

Calico Fabric Shop
52 Main Street
Florence, MA 01062
413-585-8665
www.calicofabric.com
Over 3,000 bolts of fabric for
all your decorating needs.

The Color Wheel Company
541-929-7526
www.colorwheelco.com
Color wheels to help you
match tints, tones, and
shades.

Crate & Barrel
646 N Michigan Avenue
Chicago, IL 60611
800-996-9960
www.crateandbarrel.com
An excellent source of
good-value furniture and
accessories.

Décor Color
2820 T.O. Boulevard
Thousand Oaks, CA 91362
805-495-7097
www.decorcolor.com
Range of unique and difficult-
to-find paint products. Holds
faux finishing classes.

Duralee Fabric Factory Outlet
1775 Fifth Avenue
Brentwood, NY 11717
631-273-8800
Known for traditional designs
in fashionable colorations.

Fabrics To Dye For
Two River Road
Pawcatuck, CT 06379
800-322-1319
www.fabricstodyefor.com
Hand-painted fabrics, dyes,
and kits; also available from
various retail outlets.

Factory Paint and Decorating
55 Washington Street
Pembroke, MA 02358
800-696-3400
www.gis.net/~fps/
Home improvement through
wall coverings, paint, and
interior design.

Farrow & Ball Inc.
845-369-4912
www.farrow-ball.com
Historic paints.

Gracious Home
1220 Third Avenue
New York, NY 10021
212-517-6300
Hardware, paints, varnishes.

Hancock Fabrics
2605A West Main Street
Tupelo, MS 38801
662-844-7368
www.hancockfabrics.com
Largest US fabric store; good
for all basic decoration needs.

Home Depot
1520 New Brighton Boulevard
Minneapolis, MN 55413
612-782-9594
www.homedepot.com
Provides equipment and
supplies for every type of
home DIY project, locations
throughout the country.

IKEA
1800 East McConnor
Parkway
Schaumburg, IL 60173
www.ikea.com
Home basics at great prices.

Janovic
1150 Third Avenue
New York, NY 10021
800-772-4381
www.janovic.com
A quality selection of paints in
a wide color range.

Krylon
800-4KRYLON
www.krylon.com
General-purpose paints,
primers, enamels, and latex;
specialty paints; crackle
paints, stone effects.

Laura Ashley Home Store
171 East Ridgewood Avenue
Ridgewood, NJ 07450
201-670-0686
www.laura-ashleyusa.com
Floral, striped, checked, and
solid cottons in many colors.

Lowe's
3909 Ramsey Street
Fayetteville, NC 28311
877-235-0073
www.lowes.com
Home improvement
warehouse, with paints
and wallcoverings.

Lunn Fabrics Ltd.
317 East Main Street
Lancaster, OH 43130-3845
800-880-1738
www.lunnfabrics.com
One-of-a-kind hand-dyed and
painted fabrics in every color
and design.

Pier One Imports
71 Fifth Avenue
New York, NY 10003
212-206-1911
www.pier1.com
Wonderful selection of
affordable and stylish drapes
and curtains.

Pottery Barn
600 Broadway
New York, NY 10012
800-922-5507
www.potterybarn.com
Everything from furniture to
decoration details, such as
muslin curtains, china, pillows,
and candlesticks.

Pratt & Lambert Paints
800-BUY-PRATT
www.prattandlambert.com
Creator of Accolade paint
products; interior and exterior
paints, flat, satin, enamel, and
distinctive faux finishes.

Ralph Lauren Paint Collection
At Ralph Lauren
867 Madison Avenue
New York, NY 10021
212-606-2100
Signature collection of colors
grouped in romantic themes
such as River Rock and
Desert Hollywood.

Reprodepot Fabrics
6523 California Avenue
SW, PMB 272
Seattle, WA 98136-1879
206-938-5585
www.reprodepotfabrics.com
Individually designed cotton
fabrics in fun colors and
designs for nurseries,
toddlers, and creative uses.

Restoration Hardware
The Atrium
300 Boylston Street
Chestnut Hill
MA 02467-1922
617-641-6770
www.restorationhardware.com
Funky home furnishings,
lighting, and accessories.

Sherwin Williams
4333 Kent Road
Stow, OH 44224
330-688-3088
www.sherwin.com
Multi-product DIY interior
decoration store; locations
throughout the country.

Sydney Harbor Paint Co.
12602 Ventura Boulevard
Studio City, CA 91604
818-623-9394
www.porterspaints.com
Finest ingredients and original
recipes used to make durable
paints and finishes such as
lime wash, acrylics, satins,
glazes, and many more.

Waverly
800-423-5881
www.waverly.com
On-line store. Decorative
accessories including fabric,
wallpaper, furniture, window
treatments, tabletop, paint,
and floor coverings.

West Elm
P.O. Box 29028
Brooklyn, NY 11202-9028
866-428-6468
www.westelm.com
Features laid-back modernism
with Asian-inspired colors.

credits

Key a = above, **b** = below, **r** = right, **l** = left, **c** = center.

Front jacket Alan Williams/Richard Oyarzarbal's apartment in London designed by Urban Research Laboratory. **Back jacket** Above left, right and below right Debi Treloar; above centre Tom Leighton; below left and centre left Ray Main; below centre right Alan Williams/The architect Voon Wong's own apartment in London

Endpapers ph Debi Treloar/Anna Massee of Het Grote Avontuur (The Great Adventure)'s home in Amsterdam; **1** ph Chris Everard/Pemper and Rabiner home in New York, designed by David Khouri of Comma; **2** ph Debi Treloar/Anna Massee of Het Grote Avontuur (The Great Adventure)'s home in Amsterdam; **3** ph Debi Treloar/The home of Studio Aandacht. Design by Ben Lambers; **4l** ph Christopher Drake/Fay & Roger Oates' house in Ledbury; **4c** Henry Bourne/floor by Dalsouple, First Floor; **4r** ph Tom Leighton/bowls Julie Goodwin; **5** ph Jan Baldwin/Claire Haithwaite and Dean Maryon's home in Amsterdam; **6–7** ph Tom Leighton; **8a** ph Andrew Wood/Nanna Ditzel's home in Copenhagen; **8b** ph James Merrell; **9** Colour Wheel © The Color Wheel Company (www.colorwheelco.com, t. 541 929 7526); **10a** ph Alan Williams/Andrew Wallace's house in London; **10b** ph Alan Williams/The Arbuthnott family's house near Cirencester designed by Nicholas Arbuthnott, fabrics designed by Vanessa Arbuthnott; **11** ph Christopher Drake/Juan Corbella'a apartment in London designed by HM2, Richard Webb with Andrew Hanson; **12a** ph Polly Wreford/Marie-Hélène de Taillac's pied-à-terre in Paris; **12b** ph Chris Everard/Mark Weinstein's apartment in New York designed by Lloyd Schwan; **13a** ph Tom Leighton; **13b** ph Christopher Drake/Designer Barbara Davis' own house in upstate New York; **14** ph Simon Upton/Conner Prairie; **15bl** ph Alan Williams/Alannah Weston's house in London designed by Stickland Coombe Architecture; **15a & bc** ph Alan Williams; **15r** ph Debi Treloar; **16–17** ph Debi Treloar/Debi Treloar's family home in north-west London; **18** ph Jan Baldwin/The Meiré family home, designed by Marc Meiré; **19l** ph Debi Treloar; **19r** ph Debi Treloar/The home of Patty Collister in London, owner of An Angel At My Table; **20l** ph Jan Baldwin/Jan Hashey and Yasuo Minagawa; **20r** ph Jan Baldwin/The Meiré family home, designed by Marc Meiré; **21al & r** ph Tom Leighton; **21cl & bl** ph Christopher Drake/Nordic Style Kitchen; **22al** ph Debi Treloar/North London flat of presentation skills trainer/actress and her teacher husband, designed by Gordana Mandic of Buildburo; **22bl** ph Debi Treloar/Nicky Phillips' apartment in London; **22br** ph Debi Treloar/Clare and David Mannix-Andrews' house, Hove, East Sussex; **23a** ph Jan Baldwin/A family home in Parsons Green, London. Architecture by Nicholas Helm and Yasuyuki Fukuda (architectural assistant) of Helm Architects. Interior design and all material finishes supplied by Maria Speake of Retrouvius Reclamation & Design; **23bl & c** ph Tom Leighton; **23br** ph Debi Treloar/Mark and Sally of Baileys Home and Garden's house in Herefordshire; **24l** ph Andrew Wood/Mary Shaw's Sequana apartment in Paris; **24r** ph Christopher Drake/A house in Salisbury designed by Helen Ellery of The Plot London; **25ar** ph Jan Baldwin/The Fitzwilliam-Lay's family home. Architecture by Totem Design, interior design by Henri Fitzwilliam-Lay and Totem Design; **25b** ph Debi Treloar/Mark and Sally of Baileys Home and Garden's house in Herefordshire; **26a** ph Debi Treloar/A London apartment designed by James Soane and Christopher Ash of Project Orange; **26b** ph Tom Leighton; **27** ph Chris Everard/An actor's London home designed by Site Specific; **28a** ph Catherine Gratwicke; **28b** ph Jan Baldwin/Wendy Jansen and Chris Van Eldik, owners of J.O.B. Interieur's house in Wijk bij Duurstede, The Netherlands; **29** ph Chris Everard/designed by Mullman Seidman Architects; **29r** ph Jan Baldwin/Alfredo Paredes and Brad Goldfarb's loft in Tribeca, New York designed by Michael Neumann Architecture; **30a** ph Chris Everard/A New York apartment designed by Shamir Shah. Paintings, Artist Malcolm Hill; **30bl** ph Debi Treloar/Mark and Sally of Baileys Home and Garden's house in Herefordshire; **30br** ph Christopher Drake/Florence Lim's house in London – architecture by Voon Wong Architects, interior design by Florence Lim Design; **31** ph Tom Leighton/A house in London designed by Charles Rutherfoord, 51 The Chase, London SW4 0NP, UK, + 44 20 7627 0182; **32al** ph Tom Leighton; **32bl** ph Jan Baldwin/Alfredo Paredes and Brad Goldfarb's loft in Tribeca, New York designed by Michael Neumann Architecture; **32ar** ph Alan Williams/The architect Voon Wong's own apartment in London; **32br** ph Alan Williams/Alannah Weston's house in London designed by Stickland Coombe Architecture; **33l** ph Christopher Drake/A house designed by artist Angela A'Court, extension and alteration to rear of property by S.I. Robertson at 23 Architecture; **33ar** ph Jan Baldwin/The Campbell family's apartment in London, architecture by Voon Wong Architects; **33br** ph Tom Leighton; **34** ph Henry Bourne/John Raab's apartment in London/floor by Sinclair Till; **35ar** ph Debi Treloar/Artist David Hopkins' house in East London, designed by Yen-Yen Teh of Emulsion; **35bl** James Merrell/A house in Sydney designed by Interni Interior Design Consultancy; **35c** ph Christopher Drake/Juan Corbella'a apartment in London designed by HM2, Richard Webb with Andrew Hanson; **35r** ph Alan Williams/Owner of Gloss, Pascale Bredillet's own apartment in London; **36al** ph Alan Williams/Margot Feldman's house in New York designed by Patricia Seidman of Mullman Seidman Architects; **36ar** ph Alan Williams/Interior Designer and Managing Director of the Société Yves Halard, Michelle Halard's own apartment in Paris; **36br** ph Tom Leighton; **37** ph Debi Treloar/The home of Studio Aandacht. Design by Ben Lambers; **38l** ph Tom Leighton/A house in London designed by Charles Rutherfoord, 51 The Chase, London SW4 0NP, UK, + 44 20 7627 0182 — vase & beaker by Edmund de Waal, table Nordic Style; **38–39** ph Jan Baldwin/Claire Haithwaite and Dean Maryon's home in Amsterdam; **39ar** ph Alan Williams/The Arbuthnott family's house near Cirencester designed by Nicholas Arbuthnott, fabrics designed by Vanessa Arbuthnott; **39b** ph Alan Williams/Maria Jesus Polanco's apartment in New York designed by Hut Sachs

Studio in collaboration with Moneo Brock Studio; **40** ph Alan Williams/Richard Oyarzarbal's apartment in London designed by Urban Research Laboratory; **41l** ph Tom Leighton; **41r** ph Alan Williams/The architect Voon Wong's own apartment in London; **42l** ph Christopher Drake/John Minshaw's house in London; **42r** ph Tom Leighton; **43l** ph Polly Wreford/Lena Proudlock's house in Gloucestershire; **43ar** ph Ray Main/Evan Snyderman's house in Brooklyn; **43br & 44** ph Alan Williams/Selworthy apartment in London designed by Gordana Mandic & Peter Tyler at Buildboro (www.buildboro.co.uk); **45l** ph Debi Treloar/Susan Cropper's family home in London —www.63hlg.com; **45r** ph Tom Leighton; **46l** ph Alan Williams/Warner Johnson's apartment in New York designed by Edward Cabot of Cabot Design Ltd.; **46r** ph Chris Everard/John Barman's Park Avenue Apartment; **47l** ph Alan Williams/Jennifer & Geoffrey Symonds' apartment in New York designed by Jennifer Post Design; **47r** ph Alan Williams/Director of design consultants Graven Images, Janice Kirkpatrick's apartment in Glasgow; **48al** ph Debi Treloar; **48bl** ph Alan Williams/Lindsay Taylor's apartment in Glasgow; **48ar** ph Debi Treloar/The home of Studio Aandacht. Design by Ben Lambers; **48br** ph Alan Williams; **49** ph Debi Treloar; **49bl** ph Debi Treloar/Clare and David Mannix-Andrews' house, Hove, East Sussex; **49r** ph Debi Treloar/Susan Cropper's family home in London—www.63hlg.com; **50** ph Alan Williams/Lindsay Taylor's

apartment in Glasgow; **51l** ph Jan Baldwin/Claire Haithwaite and Dean Maryon's home in Amsterdam; **51r** ph Christopher Drake; **52l** ph Tom Leighton/Sally Butler's house in London; **52ar** ph Catherine Gratwicke; **52br** ph Christopher Drake/William Yeoward and Colin Orchard's home in London; **53l** ph Alan Williams/Donata Sartorio's apartment in Milan; **53r** ph James Merrell/Sally Butler's house in London; **54** ph Alan Williams/Private apartment in London designed by Hugh Broughton Architects; **55a** ph Alan Williams/Interior Designer John Barman's own apartment in New York; **55b** ph Ray Main/lighting by Tsé Tsé associées, Catherine Levy and Sigolène Prébois; **56bl** ph Tom Leighton/Roger & Fay Oates' house in Herefordshire, The Long Barn, Eastnor, Ledbury, Herefordshire HR8 1EL, + 44 1531 632718; **56ar** ph Debi Treloar/The home of Studio Aandacht. Design by Ben Lambers; **57l** ph Ray Main/Seth Stein's house in London, light by Erco; **57r** ph Debi Treloar/Debi Treloar's family home in north-west London; **58al & ar** ph Alan Williams/Richard Oyarzarbal's apartment in London designed by Urban Research Laboratory; **58bl & br** ph Alan Williams/Private apartment in London designed by Hugh Broughton Architects; **59al** ph Simon Upton; **59ar** ph Chris Everard/Apartment of Amy Harte Hossfeld and Martin Hossfeld; **59bl** ph James Merrell/Vicky and Simon Young's house in Northumberland; **59br** ph Debi Treloar/Ian Hogarth's family home

Architects and designers whose work is featured in this book

23 Architecture
S.I. Robertson
www.23arc.com
Page 33l.

27.12 Design Ltd
www.2712design.com
Page 59ar.

An Angel At My Table
Painted furniture and accessories
+ 44 20 7424 9777
and
+ 44 1799 528777
Page 19r.

Angela A'Court, Artist
Orangedawe@hotmail.com
Page 33l.

Baileys Home & Garden
www.baileyshomeandgarden.com
Pages 23br, 25b, 30bl.

buildburo ltd
www.buildburo.co.uk
Pages 22al, 43br & 44.

Cabot Design Ltd
Interior Design
212 222 9488
eocabot@aol.com
Page 46l.

The Color Wheel Company
www.colorwheelco.com
541 929 7526
Page 9.

Comma
www.comma-nyc.com
Page 1.

Conner Prairie
134000 Alisonville Road
Fishers
Indiana 46038
www.connerprairie.com
Page 14.

Barbara Davis
Interior design; antique hand-dyed linen, wool and silk textiles by the yard; soft furnishings and clothes to order.
607 264 3673
Page 13b.

Emulsion
www.emulsionarchitecture.com
Page 35ar.

Gloss Ltd
Designers of home accessories
+ 44 20 8960 4146
pascale@glossltd.u-net.com
Pages 35r.

Helen Ellery of The Plot London
www.theplotlondon.com
Page 24r.

Henri Fitzwilliam-Lay
Interior Design
Hfitz@hotmail.com
Page 25ar.

Het Grote Avontuur
www.hetgroteavontuur.nl
Pages Endpapers, 2.

HM2 Architects
Architects and designers
www.harper-mackay.co.uk
Pages 11, 35c.

Helm Architects
nh@helmarchitects.com
Page 23a.

Hugh Broughton Architects
Award-winning architects
+ 44 20 7602 8840
hugh@hbarchitects.demon.co.uk
Pages 54, 58bl & br.

Hut Sachs Studio
Architecture and interior design
212 219 1567
www.hutsachs.com
Page 39b.

Interni Pty Ltd
Interior design consultancy
15–19 Boundary Street
Rushcutter's Bay
Sydney 2010
Australia
Page 35bl.

J.O.B. Interieur
+ 31 343 578818
JOBINT@xs4all.nl
Page 28b.

Jennifer Post Design Inc.
Spatial and interior designer
212 734 7994
jpostdesign@aol.com
Page 47l.

John Barman Inc.
Interior design and decoration
www.johnbarman.com
Page 46r, 55a.

John Minshaw Designs Ltd
Enquiries@johnminshawdesigns.com
Page 42l.

Lena Proudlock
www.deniminstyle.com
Page 43l.

Littman Goddard Hogarth
www.lgh-architects.co.uk
Page 59br.

Lloyd Schwan/Design
212 375 0858
lloydschwan@earthlink.net
Page 12b.

Marc Meiré
Meirefamily@aol.com
Pages 18, 20r.

Michael Neumann Architecture
www.mnarch.com
Pages 29r, 32bl.

Moneo Brock Studio
www.moneobrock.com
Page 39b.

Mullman Seidman Architects
Architecture and interior design
www.mullmanseidman.com
Pages 29, 36al.

Nanna Ditzel MDD FCSD
Industrial designer specializing
in furniture, textiles, jewellery
and exhibitions.
www.nanna-ditzel-design.dk
Page 8a.

Nordic Style
Classic Swedish interiors
109 Lots Road
London SW10 ORN, UK
Pages 21cl & bl.

Nicholas Arbuthnott
Arbuthnott Ladenbury Architects
Architects and urban designers
15 Gosditch Streetv
Cirencester GL7 2AG, UK
Page 10b, 39ar.

Project Orange
www.projectorange.com
Page 26a.

Retrouvius Reclamation & Design
www.retrouvius.com
Page 23a.

Roger Oates Design
shop and showroom
1 Munro Terrace
off Cheyne Walk
London SW10 ODL, UK
studio shop
The Long Barn
Eastnor, Ledbury
Herefordshire HR8 1EL, UK
Page 4l, 56bl..

Rugs & Runners
Mail-order catalog
+ 44 1531 631611
Pages 4l, 56bl.

SAD Interiors
+ 44 7930 626916
sad@flymedia.co.uk
Page 35ar.

Scquana
+ 33 1 45 66 58 40
sequana@wanadoo.fr
Page 24l.

Shamir Shah
Shahdesign@earthlink.net
Page 30a.

Site Specific Ltd
www.sitespecificltd.co.uk
Page 27.

Seth Stein
Architect
+ 44 20 8968 8581
Page 57l.

Stickland Coombe Architecture
+ 44 20 7924 1699
nick@scadesign.freeserve.co.uk
Pages 15bl, 32br.

Studio Aandacht
Art direction and interior production
www.studioaandacht.nl
Pages 3, 37, 48ar, 56ar.

Totem Design
Ian Hume
+ 44 20 7243 0692
totem.uk@virgin.net
Page 25ar.

Urban Research Laboratory
Architects
+ 44 20 7403 2929
jeff@urbanresearchlab.com
Pages 40, 58al & ar.

Vanessa Arbuthnott Fabrics
www.vanessaarbuthnott.co.uk
Page 10b, 39ar.

Voon Wong Architects
+ 44 20 7587 0116
voon@btconnect.com
Page 30br, 32ar, 33ar, 41r.

William Yeoward
270 Kings Road
London SW3 5AW, UK
+ 44 20 7349 7828
www.williamyeoward.com
Page 52br.

Yves Halard
Interior decoration
+ 33 1 42 22 60 50
Page 36ar.

index

Italics indicate picture captions.